CW01508968

Conscious
Conversations

First paperback edition February 2023

Book design by Bee

ISBN 9798373969208 (paperback)

Special thank you to my good friend Bee who designed the book cover. A final thank you to everyone who broke me, helped me heal and made me realise the beauty and pain that comes with love; the words wouldn't be on the pages without you.

VULNERABILITY

TOLL

STRENGTH

HOLDING ONTO

FORGIVING AND CHOSING KINDNESS

QUESTIONING

6. *SILENT SIGNALS (BOB DYLAN)*
7. *YOU'RE NOT HOME*
8. *I WISH IT HAD KILLED YOU*
9. *IS THIS THE TIME YOU DON'T COME BACK?*
10. *TO TRY GET CLOSE TO YOU*
11. *CURED THE WORDS*
12. *QUESTIONING*
13. *SOMETHING ISNT RIGHT*
14. *I DON'T KNOW WHAT YOU THINK OF WHEN YOU THINK OF ME*
15. *STALLING*
16. *ALCOHOL FREE BEER*
17. *HOPE HE KNOWS WE'RE OUT TONIGHT*
18. *I WISH YOU WERE A PHONE GUY.*

VULNERABILITY.

*Times I have been open and honest with myself,
allowing my body to flow with my emotions and not
be embarrassed to feel the way I feel. Everyone has a
vulnerable side, but letting others access this
vulnerability can lead to chaos or hope for those who
read. My wounds are open, my blood lies on these
pages. Here it is, vulnerability.*

I'm a traveller,
my body is elsewhere when
I'm in the room, physically.
my fingers are numb and cold,
my feet unable to move,
stuck in the mud,
unable to function without
thinking of you.
now my heart
has made its way through
to my throat
and has me in a chokehold
so, I spit out the words that
they have to say to you
because I don't think with
my head when I speak because
emotions overrule actions sometimes.
you have your hands so
conveniently under my chin
because you already know what
I'm about to say, and
I hate that.
-how can you read my mind but
not read how I'm feeling.

I am so scared to let go

I am so scared to let go
and I don't know how to
free myself from the
invisible barricades that cage me in
with nuts and bolts that are made from
thin air but they have me
in a chokehold
dancing with my past
taunting in front of my eyes
laughing at my sickened self
who is prescribed one tablet a day
of the past
and I take it with
more than one sip
of unbranded vodka that I
filled half with water when I was
14 years old and
going to a party
I am banished in the past
and everything reminds me
of reasons I wanted to be me instead of
being who I am right now.

my biggest fear is
my room setting on fire when nobody's here
so how can I make
all my love letters that I wrote from
-*my hearts feelings*-
how can I make sure people get those?
I want people to know
what I very truly feel like about them
especially you herb
so, what can I do to make sure
that it'll be saved
if I was to ever have a house fire?
no fireproof boxes?
but surely not everything sets on fire?
there has to be something
that can make it through a fire?
please?
I got stuff I need to make it through fires

at least I'm touching you

the very first time we met, you pushed me into the snow, we laughed for hours and my ankle hurt a little the next day but at least we were touching. I remember when we used to wind the windows down and sing baby in the car, shouting 'we're just friends, what are you saying' whilst holding each other's hands, platonically, but at least we were touching. that day I failed the bet, we met up the next day and our lips locked for what felt like a lifetime, and I was so close touching this time, almost as if we were one human in two forms. and it happened again, and again, and yet again, every time becoming more of eachother in the most perfect and special way. And it had suddenly led to my cold feet on your warm back, and you hated it but at least we were still touching. But then you left.

Although we are not touching, the electricity somehow keeps us magnetised from every glimpse of each other that we catch. The energy you had brought into my life will never leave, like the smell of fresh cut grass, the feeling of fuzzy warm winter socks, the taste that wine leaves in your mouth. you spark something in me that will not stop flickering and that is enough for me to think we will still touch even if you're elsewhere. I know we're no longer touching but at least I had once touched.

I feel like a man in a skirt

I don't know if that's because
my legs are built quite funny
or that my jumper comes too long
or maybe the fact I don't chose to
shave my legs because
it's way too much energy
and I have none of that.
I feel like a man in a skirt
and I've felt like this for a long time
but when I'm naked and I
look at myself in the mirror
I'm a woman and I *feel* like a woman
however today? I don't know why?
I feel like a man in a skirt
sometimes I feel like a girl in tracksuits
but not as much as I can't explain
as to why I feel like a man in a skirt
and maybe I don't know
I feel masculine about the way I look today?
but I feel masculine most days
even if I'm wearing a dress
or wearing a jumpsuit
today I really feel like I am a man
and I look at myself in the long stretch mirror
and I stand and think to myself
fuck.
I am a man today. will I be a man tomorrow?

I never knew what it was
about being afraid of pretty boys
maybe idolised the fact that
you in my eyes
could simply not compare
to the way I viewed the
worth of myself
but now I have the chance
to hold a *pretty boy;*
in the kitchen
on the sofa
entangled into your arms
left hand tucked behind my head
as though I was
the blueprint that shaped your future
you had your heart on your sleeve
and I've already promised I won't
break it
because I only get one shot
at being with a pretty boy
I swear that I won't waste it.

I laid down every single card on the table and put my hands back in my pockets. I held the inside of my thighs through my shorts and waited patiently in the silence until your gazed fixed mine. I couldn't hold back the tears from brimming my eyes, I felt like without you I think I drive myself insane because the paths aren't solid, and the roads have sinkholes which spiral to the core of the earth. it's empty here, I can't stop asking why you haven't spoken, or why your eyes can't meet to mine once I've told you how I feel. you don't have to tell me because your face is painted like the Mona Lisa, as though I already know what you're thinking, what you're going to say, how you'll react to me. it's absolutely killing me inside. you're holding the paintbrush and choosing to create and colour yourself through the words of manipulation that spill from your sentences like overflowing coffee cups. they've stained the surface they were placed on; they won't come off no matter how hard I scrub at them. I can't get away from anything, your mirages have *photocopied themselves into the grooves of my brain* and they're burning my hippocampus; with that, my memory fades into nothing but smears and blurs of us. your lips look nothing like they used to, and your voice doesn't sound so smooth anymore, you didn't just swallow grit, but your pride went along with it. sometimes it hurts to be the honest person in situations, but it's better to be honest then camouflage emotions with wrapping paper and bows. I only liked the version of you that you pretended to be.

It's as though I don't exist in your life. we take pictures, have fun times and spend half of our living breathing moments together. But I'm now where to be seen. your friends think we're friends and I feel hidden away from everything that I shouldn't be hidden from. I'm introduced to nobody and I hold myself accountable for this, but I don't like the way you expect me to blend to the background when you know you'd rather be elsewhere. I'm not asking you to change because I won't force that on you but I'm asking just for a little bit of something to make me realise I do exist. *I am human and I would like to be loved.*

I love you so much.

You're so brave, charismatic, and maybe I need to realise that is because I love you. I love you. Spoon feed me with your affection, buy me flowers, put the smile on my face. I love how you were created even if you don't, the scarring on your back from where the ache made its home even down to the way you cuff your cargo pants at the bottoms. I love you and I really mean that. *You are the most perfect example of a human being I could've ever have known.* I didn't ever realise how beautiful you are until the snowflakes danced in the reflection of your eyes that cold February morning. You were the person and will always be the person I want around in my life, whether that means we must be just friends to keep you around. I want you to be a part of my life for the rest of it, however long or short it may be, I want you to be adored like you deserve and I want you to realise how amazing you truly are.

the fact we go from
talking every day
talking every second
unable to function without
each other's physical touch and now
we can't even make eye contact
without feeling awkward
or have a conversation without
twiddling thumbs
now your safety nets
have loopholes
and your tightropes
are fraying
why do I feel
that I'm
forever in your debt.

I miss your blonde coil curls
and the way you lie in bed
and your eyes as blue as oceans
thinking while lying in my bed
how could you break me down so much?
that I can sometimes think your here
when you're instead out with her
something I knew I'd always fear
and now I wake up in the mornings
feeling cold and all alone
because you never truly loved me
your dishonestly drove me crazy
and your mums a fucking liar
who brought me to tears.
valentine's day didn't even feel like
valentine's day
it felt like I was about to watch you play
call of duty on my own
begging that you'd
ask if I wanted to play too
but you never did.

you'd had your hand in my hair so many times
I sometimes wake up and feel it there
but then I realise I'm alone in my
three quarter bed that's cold and lonely
when I know you're elsewhere with
whoever you're choosing to be with tonight
just for the fact that you can.
I could never hate you
For what you chose to do
But that doesn't mean it
Doesn't stab me square in the chest
Whenever I think of you.

you are
exactly who you
said you wouldn't be
and isn't that a shame
isn't it a shame?
that all our plans
a future we could've built
was put out as
forged signatures
forced I love you's
faked affection.
I would hurt myself
1000 times over to
just have felt what
you felt
so I wasn't the only
one who believed
that I was in love.

a pretty face
doesn't always mean
a pretty heart,
so, when will it be my turn
to be the holder?
how can I keep holding on?
how can we keep holding on?
please stop putting your
flame covered hands on
my paper thin heart;
you are bound to
be the arsonist
that alights
the burning embers
that lie as carpet
in my heart.

chase not attract

I'm not a runner
my lungs are frayed from all the
late night smokes
clearing my brain from the world
so why am I running to you at
every given opportunity when I know
I don't run.
Maybe you're worth the
Leg cramps and sport sickness
That I constantly put myself through
To try and catch your attention
Just because I want you to see me
Exactly how I see you.

I'm trying to let you in,
I am, as a friend.
I somehow managed to
Build trust with you
And within microseconds
My heart fell through
The souls of the shoes that were
Walking me to the safe spot
I thought I'd found within you,
Which turned out to end
In a dungeon of
Misleading words and
False propositions.
Were you ever even interested?
In taking me out or
Did you just want another mark
For your scoreboard?
I wanted to know you more
Than a launchpad and a flower wall.
I. wanted. to. be. your. friend.
But now I'm left
So very, very confused.
Crazy how a girl who
Never has felt any type of
Outside attention
Puts her trust into someone
Who sends her a message
To feel instantly lied to.
What a vulnerable little girl I am.

I'm tired of crying myself to sleep every night, stroking the sides of my face with the insides of my thumb, holding myself because I need the touch, I'm just tired of it. Truth is the only person I knew how to love was you. you broke me, and although you don't think you did, you made me believe I was going crazy, that you didn't do what you did do and although I can't prove you did it, *things didn't line up.* I wish that you could've been it. I wish it was us like we planned. Instead, I'm searching for comfort in others that don't love me like you did. I'd take back every bad thing to just relive the happiness in any of our single moments together. I would go through the pain 10 times over just to hold your hand one last time.

it's the
kissing at the red light
type of love
the type where every glimpse
is tension
not just sexual but
magnetic.
attracted.
mirrors image
of what we should be
compared to how we're living
isn't even close to
what we want.
your hand placed
so comfortably over my
hand on the gearstick
as though it never left
as though *you* never left.
what is the point in leaving
when you've
never even left.

I sit and cry about you whilst in somebody else's arms. I thought I could be over you but for some reason it's getting harder to push aside. I hate what you did to me, I hate it more than anything, but it doesn't mean I hate you. you had your reasons to break me, and I must be able to forgive you for that if I can bring myself to miss you, and I do, so somewhere in my brain has accepted the pain and wants to look past it. *I miss you.* I miss you more than anything, and instead my heart has led me elsewhere so I can be looked after until you admit you miss me too. I don't know how long I can wait for that; I don't know what you truly did and I don't know if I will ever 100% forgive you.

mistakes aren't mistakes
when you refuse
to say
sorry.
the toxicity of the words you spoke
so manipulative yet so soothing
I believed that you wanted to save me
yet I was drowning still after
your meaningless sorry sob story
how you never felt right
yet you'd allow me no room to breathe
and it's as though I'm
suffocating
being trapped in some sort of
bubble with you.
no air.
crushing my chest.
you'd think that
weighing only 60kg I could cope
but after a while
it became some sort of ache
and I was too weak
to allow you to break me breathless.
to shatter not only my rib cage
but caverns of my heart
were pierced with my own bones
and now I'm repairing myself
from wounds inflicted by you
-I only hurt myself.

7 month probation period

can I picture us
browsing the crisp isle
in a different country
the sun in our eyes
watermelon skies
snaps around the pool
ice cream in our hands.
I wish I could.
but it seems I never leave
that 7 month probation period
I must just get bored of
the loss of attention
or the fear of attachment
or the lack of commitment
possibly just a fraction
of what we had just gone
in a foreign country
singing the catchy tune in the
local mercadonna
is where we could be
if I could ever
make it past 7 months.
-the things I'd do to find the right person.

I have hidden hurt
from things I can't discuss
because I don't know how to
I am always left
to pick up the pieces of
your mistakes and
regardless of how much
I tell you how I feel
about you doing what you do
you never really take
into consideration
me having to clean up your mess
that you cause unknowingly
meaning I'm left with
all of this
submerged trauma
that I don't know how to talk about
so instead I try communicating
in the morning
and you still don't thank me
for repeatedly
saving your stupid life.

Make believe

I can't now travel on your side of the room. you never came here, so this was a metaphorical start, but it has its reason. When I first started to talk to you, I would question how far you actually were from me. I would go on google maps and see the distance between us and see the direction that you were to me. For my room, this was the corner of the house that my front door was. I'd face your direction when id send you a message, hoping this could make us feel closer but it just never did. It passed the stage where I'd not even think about and subconsciously would walk in the parts where I was closest to you and facing your direction.

I realised I liked you
when we were in the hills
sheltered by the trees
looking over where we live
pointing to places
that we could make out
even though it's pitch black.
but now the memories
are faded- pitch black.
I miss you
but one day
our love will still lie
resting on the hills
we're under the trees
yes- *still*
but this time
we happen to be
six feet under I realised I like you
when we were in the hills
sheltered by the trees
looking over where we live
pointing to places
that we could make out
even though it's pitch black.
but now the memories
are faded- pitch black.
I miss you
but one day
our love will still lie

I was something you wanted
but I wasn't a need
a necessity
you liked the control you had
when you knew when I was
at my weakest
I would claw myself back to your feet
and beg for your love through
stolen tears because I
regret never telling you that
I rely on you for my happiness
when I wish
I never did. *but I still do*.

Hairs cover your eyes as they
Taunt with your lips but
That's only where I wish mine were
pressed;
Upon yours, but when the sun
Comes up and creeps from
Behind the curtain I begin to see
Your flushed cheeks and its
Not because you're warm but
Because I had you lay next to me
Crying into your pillow whilst I slept
through
The thunderstorm and you chose not to
Wake me up because you believed that
I was -*or am*- like the people
You've previously broke down around.
I regret the fact I never just held you
Instead, I froze until you left the room
       I'm sorry I couldn't handle the
       situation.

it doesn't matter
where I am
I can always crave
your arms around me
you're my jacket
your arms on my hips
you're my guide
your arms on my shoulders
you're my muse.
there's something about
your touch
that makes me believe
that you could
never hurt me
and for that I am
applauding a dog for walking
but in this cruel world
it's rare to find
someone like you.

grief is a ghost.

grief is a ghost
that sleeps underneath your covers
and whistles with the kettle
while you make yourself a drink
and it doesn't knock,
it doesn't ask permission
instead, it lingers in all of your
passing days like a
shroud above you
and allows itself to create a
tornado that tears through
the muscles in your body
and pulls them until you ache

grief is a ghost
that meets you halfway in the swimming pool
that grabs your feet and pulls you under
and it doesn't care
that you're a strong swimmer,
it doesn't allow you to float
instead, you drown under the
chlorine water that was
changed 6 months ago
and that 6 months changed your life

grief is a ghost
that sits beside your bedside table
hides within the clothes in your wardrobe
and every time you're getting changed

you catch a glimpse of the grief
that you wear like a warm woolly coat
keeps you warm but also gets too hot
and when it
gets too hot it gets
too heavy
you're suffocating in your grief

grief is a ghost
that lurks within the trees
and buries itself in our back gardens
deep under the ground
and sometimes it stops growing,
in the colder months, grief may not be there
it might instead disguise itself as a
bonsai tree that's lost its leaves
and sometimes we smile
at the progress it makes.

grief isn't linear
and it comes and goes
like leaving your house for work
it's like a stranger in your home
or your lifeless body in a pool
or a coat you wear in winter
it's like a plant you don't want to water
grief is a ghost
and it'll haunt you forever.

I remember
my warm tears
touch your soft lips
as we both knew
it was a final goodbye
how I wish it
could be different but
you broke me first
and now I'm left with
only being able to
put my hands
where you put yours
just to feel a touch
half as soft as yours
because I wish you were still
here with me
instead, you made
decisions I couldn't
put myself to
stand by
so here I am
choosing someone else
or something else
to ease the pain
of putting you under
and *laying the*
trilogy of the
white ferrari
to rest.

Round you I feel like
Every breath that is filling my lungs
Is stolen with every word you talk
Though our *conscious conversations*
Tampers with my heart
Each heart string that you use as
Jump ropes are now
Pulling your love tighter and
Very soon I know that I'll
Have your hands that instead
Chose to touch my soul
And show me that your
Comforting presence is
Worth every single sacrifice that I made
To be here with you tonight
Instead of tucked up in bed alone
Wishing you were here instead
But 5 hours is enough to be able to
Spend a little time and grow together as a pair
-conscious conversations

love is kissing your friends on the forehead, it's waking up super early to go sit and watch the sunrise, it's reading the same book over and over because you don't want to start anything new, it's holding onto sticky Haribo rings from special times, it's tiny little tablets that help you sleep at night, it's funny moments that we laugh until we're sick, it's holding your mums hand at the big age of 20 years old, it's facetime calls with your best friend at 3am, it's selfies on 0.5 and laughing at how big your head looks, it's stolen moments that we take for granted way too often, it's our first times of everything new, it's forgiving yourself for things you allowed to take over, it's brushing your teeth while bopping your head to harry styles, it's hanging your socks on your radiator to dry, it's skidding down the isle of the supermarket in crocs and falling over at the end. we get so caught up over what love is as a society we often forget to give it to ourselves; we forget to water the plants inside our hearts, *we forget* to smile at ourselves in the Starbucks window, we forget to spend time with ourselves to the point we lose touch of who we are. if you're going to forgive anyone today, forgive yourself.

I wish you knew how I felt about you

your melty persona
we're sat here laughing
that I'll full name you
and you feel like you're
in some type of trouble
don't worry I know you're
just being soft with me
and everyone including you
can see that you're a nice human
nice is calling me pretty girl in the mornings
nice is hearting my messages
nice is sending me goodnight messages
nice is you
I think you're nice
but like
really fucking nice
-the end

the way you tuck my hair behind my ears
and you tickle my back
once I've turned the other way.
the way you call me pretty girl,
blush at my compliments
let me rest my hands on your chest.
the way you don't like when I
rest my cold feet on your
warm back in the winter,
the way you tell me to look away
whilst you get changed
like I haven't seen it all before,
the way you tuck me in
to make sure I'm okay
and kiss my neck goodnight.
we're intertwined lovers
or two lovers intertwined
but you don't really like the smiths.
I would give you everything
if you'd just let me show you
how I can love now that
a silly little pill has
completely fulfilled my life
and I am the most caring
most compassionate and passionate
person that I can be.
I love you so much
and one day I long for you to
say you love me too.

I'm not worthy of the love
From everyone and anyone
I am not made to be loved,
Nourished, cared for, taken care of.
I am meant to cause hurricanes
Car crashes, tears, heartbreak.
I don't deserve to be loved.
I am a monster
A heartless, cold, unloving human
Who can turn within seconds and
Hate your guts for no reason,
Who makes mountains our of molehills,
Who ruins everything good
Because I really do believe
I am unworthy of love.
But it doesn't mean I don't yearn for it,
That I don't ache because I'm unlovable,
It hits me every time my texts are ignored,
Every time I see my friends get married,
When I shower alone,
Or see my friends have babies,
I always am left with the label
That I can never be a human who
Is worthy of this love.

I am so scared to let go

I am so scared to let go
and I don't know how to
free myself from the
invisible barricades that cage me in
with nuts and bolts that are made from
thin air but they have me
in a chokehold
dancing with my past
taunting in front of my eyes
laughing at my sickened self
who is prescribed one tablet a day
of the past
and I take it with
more than one sip
of unbranded vodka that i
filled half with water when i was
14 years old and
going to a party
I am banished in the past
and everything reminds me
of reasons I wanted to be me instead of
being who I am right now.

TOLL

Days that have really took a toll on me mentally, the feelings that will forever exist, the feelings that don't disappear over time, that have cut me wide open and tampered with my soul's alignment, torn the contents of my memory out and branded them and the damage is irreversible. These memories make days feel heavy, fill my lungs with water and tie me down in the bottom of cold lakes, pin me up on wings of aeroplanes and bury me back in my bed. These are days that have ruined me.

how have I ended up being haunted
by something that is still on this world
living, breathing, heart still beating
as though they follow me when I
do my shopping on the noodle isle
or buy my favourite drink from Starbucks
i can't get rid of that feeling that
part of you is stuck to me
or stuck inside of me
and it's wedged so deep it's
making me think that I'm going insane thinking
you're still near me and you're
watching my every move but how
could you be watching me when
you're still a person, living, breathing
-heart still beating.

I wish we made it like we said
and that nothing on the outside mattered
just me and you alone in the world.
taking on the world.
it could be us painting fences in our garden
cleaning the kitchen in our underwear
drinking prosecco in the bath.
with *lots of bubbles.*
I don't want to hit the ground
and I wish that you held me up when
I was going to fall
instead, I'm left with bruises.
and I'm a broken woman.
cut the ropes from my hands
but please don't let me go
have Stockholm syndrome for me.
I wish we made it.

it's us again, on the dancefloor
but this time there's people between us
and it's not our skin touching
but it's yours with hers.
she's holding onto you with her
hands gripping to your biceps.
so, I drank.
and it was as though my drink was a
temporary amnesia.
you are no longer mine.
we are no longer us.
you are really gone now
and I can't see you, touch you, hold you.
hurts more than ever because
you can't wrap your arms around a memory.

from the outside it was us.
it was always us.
everything we did was together.
we had our lives mapped out
and we knew what we wanted
and one day we crumbled.
we gave in to a rough week and
it was like I'd never see you again.
but I did see you,
in fact, I still see you.
it hurts because I want you to
hold me like you used to but
I know that will never happen.
I want you to love me again
like you once did
but so much has changed since then.
they want me to believe
that you'll come back if you love me
but if you loved me then
why would you even have left.

I wasn't afraid
of getting told off
for not completing homework
or the fear that
spiders were in my room;
my fears were much more mature.
I was afraid of
losing loved ones
and knowing that
I was going through
one of the scariest things
that no nine-year-old
should ever have to experience.
I have been pulled
by my arms and legs
and stretched into
something I can't be.
-I feel hopeless
in the shoes
that are
laced around my feet.

in a parallel universe, you are here with me. we're drinking fruit shoots and laughing, you moved into our house because we couldn't bare to see you alone through the pandemic. you love seeing the dogs every day, you laugh with my mum and I've never seen her so happy, you give me a spark of hope in this world of misery. you're home, you're with us, we spent my birthday together, we didn't bring your Christmas dinner to your house you sat and ate with us. 7 places at the table. you're here with us now, February the 3rd, 6 years after you passed. you get to see me chase my dreams that you inspired me to do, you call every day and I tell you how much i love you and how grateful I am to be able to give back what paramedics gave to you. I love you. I wish we paid the line for a year so we could hear your voicemail, we gave our everything for you, you were my best friend and my bad influence, you'd always put the kettle on after a bad day or give me a Lucozade when I needed a day off school even if I wasn't poorly. you were my best friend. I miss you forever and more. *in a parallel universe,* you're still here with us.

wondering when
Baymax will just be
another big hero six
character to me
instead of being
your name
in my phone
that i still
won't allow myself
to delete.
We haven't spoken
In literal years
But I for some reason
Remember sitting in the
Computer suite
Thinking I was cool
For talking to a boy who
Was 4 years older
That myself
Little did I realise
That you were only
Grooming me.

i

who told me it gets easier?
it doesn't
I have still
lost the person that I
have ever loved the most
in this world and what can I do
to get you back
I miss you
this doesn't get easier
I am so unhappy
I miss you.

ii

I sit at my window
cracked hands upon the windowpane
wondering when the pain
will go away
as I sit where we used to
as I play the songs we painted to
as I eat the meals we used to eat
as I stroke my ears like you used to
I miss you.
I miss you way too much.
I miss you more that I thought I ever could.
I think this is
what they call
the knife of never letting go

do you still write
lame little playlists
for all the girls
you decide to
fill with hope,
tell them you love them
and that you want them
in your future
to then leave them
at the strangest times
and instead let them
listen to the songs
you've so called christened
and cry wondering
why they didn't deserve
your shitty, shitty, love.

you ask why I flinch
every time you raise your hand
but truth is I'm afraid to be
hurt again, scarred again
I don't know what love is
and every flinch is a
warning sign that puts up
barriers of do not cross tape
over the hollows of my mind.
and I tell myself you're not like him
and he would never do a thing
yet every time he tries to
hold my face I blink my eyes
that little bit harder as though he thinks
that I think he is a monster
and I'm sorry, I don't
I'm just programmed to think that
not every touch is a loving hand.

I am not bothered.
are you trying to
get under my skin?
are you trying
to make me feel
like I never meant nothing to you?
was I simply
nothing more than
a chapter
in your life?
isn't it funny how
you can really do that
to someone
you once loved?

I graze over his gaze
trying to sort my head out
knowing I want him
but can't have him.
I'm moving away.
he is not mine to love.
I can't go away
and leave him here
cold.
alone.
the guilt eats me alive.
I wish I could still love you
I wish I allowed myself
to choose you.
but your present state
has led me to believe
you no longer
feel it.
I wish I allowed myself to choose you.
but I can't.
my future depends
on being able
to leave you behind.

apparently loving you wasn't enough
I did my everything for you
I bought you extra every birthday
with my last pocket money.
yet I was still looked over
when I felt I was struggling
to even stay afloat
in a pool my feet can't touch
and it's not because I'm choosing not to.
I wish you understood me
or at least tried to.
I wish you were proud of me
I put everything on the line
just for a touch of praise.
I wish you wanted to know me
just as much
as I wish you knew me.
I wish you loved me
equally as much as you love
everyone else.

I need you
or something
to take the edge off
whatever this is I'm feeling.
a little lifter
from the letters I'm reading
at the icu
reading 'we love you and miss you'
and 'the kids think you're off working'.
I wish you knew that
my job is eating me alive
piece by piece
I will be skin and bone
and the only thing you can do
is watch in the wings and
cheer on the
creatures from the side-lines.

I'm trying to
write something
that isn't
to do with
pain
or tragedy
but it turns out
maybe these are the emotions
that represent
the way I live
and the lifestyle
I am constantly
caught up in.
I can't escape
the trauma
that is embedded
into my veins
with the
sharpest knife
writing
only they who care
will try to save you.

I can feel the happiness
I can hear it from two doors down
the speakers blaring
the floor vibrating
yet the doors are locked
and I'm stuck in the beige wash walls
I call my brain
and all it does is put up
riot shields
to stop the happiness from
breaking in
reckless intentions
and fucked up outcomes
where I lose everything I work for
and end up in bed
instead of doing things I should be doing
as my brain brews itself tired
when I'm convinced that I'm not.

you can be so
selfish with your affection
you tell me I am a priority
but manage to put
everyone who came before me
first in the line
when my whole heart is
slowly crumbling
and I'm just closer and closer
to walking through the flames
and leaving you behind
to burn
within the smoke-filled room.
now I've come to realise
my castle of trust
must've been built
with paper and fire
because as soon as
anything has been cut out
it never gets set in stone
instead, it gets burnt into flames
set alight you could say
as my walls turn to ash
and memories blow away
with the slightest sigh
-I'm exhausted from lack of trust.

assault is like a
living death note
we are alive
but at that moment
it's as though we wish
or maybe even believe
that we are dead.
I'm driving away
but you have no licence
yet you still manage
to be on my tail
and beep till I'm insane.
I did not give you permission
to parallel park in my thoughts.
it's as if you can't escape
you feel as though you
are *on the run from yourself*
I did not allow
such a vicious person
to complete marathons
in my mind.

the idea of having you to
come home to and give me
cuddles in bed when I'm half
asleep in my unclean clothes
and you're doing your sleepy voice
while I brush my hair through
seems physically impossible because
it's simply nothing but an idea
because you never seem to
fit the picture that I had
somehow painted of you and
you are forever disappointing me
with the real you
*-I loved you so much I convinced myself you were
different.*

if it wasn't your birthday
I wouldn't think twice
I'd take the blade to my skin
for one final time
I wouldn't even think about it.
if it wasn't your birthday
I'd have done it.
I can't leave your best memory
me,
creating your worst nightmare.

with you
everything feels as though
it is fairy-tale
weather it's late-night drives
to pass the time
or glimpses of you
when you've got out of the shower
to images of me
walking home with tears in my eye
flickering through personalities
trying to decide which one
        you'll chose to love today.

his smile is so genuine
and hers looks it too
I'm so scared that she'll
maybe take advantage of you
she'll treat your room like a hostel
and your heart like a rock
and even though she knows you're sad
I hope she doesn't push you past your block
that you so called had
when you were with me
and I know it's so blurry
yet so easy to see
that I can tell you want to go
and I'll never make you stay
but I just never even pictured
this was the way you'd go away

I feel my chest judder
and I already know it's going to be
you plucking at my heartstrings
using them as fishing rods
trying to reel me back in but
without a connection or a
want for me in your life.
you want me to sit around and
beg at your knees for you
and I just don't want to do that anymore
I don't want you to haunt me forever,
I want to put you in the past but you're
just not letting me do that and it's hurting me
it's hurting my so so so bad
I beg you leave quietly,
no stomping around or
ruffling with plastic bags
can you just take your shit and go?
you grabbed my heart out of my chest
and shook it about so hard
I'm now traumatised to ever try to
think about experiencing trying to fall in love again.
-thank you for ruining me.

and I thought I'd kissed my frogs
and I'd finally found my royalty
but it's nothing when loyalty
doesn't even feel real anymore
I wish you could be straight up
but you can't
and that hurts me more than
the fact you're moving on.

my heart whispers for you
and it echoes round the hollows of
my rib cage as it vibrates
sending pulses of sadness through
my body that you so called once loved
for its line work and its imperfections
that no longer exists because I scrubbed
them all away so I could live my life
without you but I know that my body
listens to my heart over my head
when it's late November night when I
want to call you at 3am and tell you
I miss you more than the moon
and the stars that shine brighter every time my
heart begs for you and you always
end the phone call because you know
exactly what is about to happen but
surely this means something to
the both of us that we are collided into
one being because we can't
live without feeding off each other's love.
-*you*

beating down the doors of my
fences that I've built
to shield me from the uproar
you brought into my life
when you decided it was done.
wood snaps and gives me
splinters in my hand
but I can't help but think
how worth it that it could be
if I allow myself to be hurt
by you.
-was it really worth it?

bonfire night

bonfire night you crushed my heart
in the palm of your hands
and wiped the remains back
onto my skin and the
fireworks were my screams
only louder than I could ever be
because I was in shock that
we had something so good
and then suddenly, we didn't
and my arms are starting to blister
from the heat of the anger that
was already in my heart for you
I wanted to physically tear off
every part of my skin
and wrap the love notes I'd wrote you
into it so you could
feel the burn whilst you
never got to read what I had to say
because you're a careless piece of work
and you don't care about
my emotions or the damage
that you caused to me that day.

STRENGTH

Times that have proved strength, from inspirational women in my life to times I have been strong and independent. Times I haven't allowed myself to be consumed with guilt, times I have been brave and not given into demons, times I have battled through hard times regardless of the hurt and confusion it may have caused along the way. Times I have been unforgivably me.

she's the woman I want to be

-yet the woman I really fear to become -

she grew in the ashes of who I used to be
which were dispersed over rose gardens
and strawberry fields that had
little white flower petals scattered
across the floor of the grass
I used to once love but sometimes
we get bored of the scene we're used to
and we want a change and become
those who made us,
so, we grow up, but the fear of
being replaced will forever exist inside
fragile paper mache hearts
we need to stop pretending to be
someone we want to be and start to
become who we are meant to be

the beauty of falling in love with yourself

because you wake up and want the most of your day
you want to appreciate your flaws
you care for yourself like no human ever could
you iron your clothes and platt your hair
you sing in the shower and paint your toes
you cook your favourite pasta for yourself
making sure to add lots of cheese because fuck the
calories
I love you for who you are Gee
the aura of smiles and radiance
that you bring to any type of mood in the room
and include people because you know what it feels
like to not be included
you are such a genuinely loveable person
just because
and one man's trash is another man's treasure
you're the spanner everyone seemed to find within
their works
Gee you are amazing. you're bloody amazing.
let go of the past and let yourself live for just once.
people admire you for who you are and if they don't
remember
this is the beauty of falling in love with yourself.

you're someone I can touch but can never hold

why can't I have you
to myself like I want?
are you sure that you don't know
that you're the love of my life.
but I don't feel like
I am yours anymore
she's just a house
and I'm more after a permanent home
you see it's as though I am
mourning the loss of someone you love
while you've synced your breathing
and you're lay right next to them
when you close your eyes
you know your home
but you've got no door keys
and you're locked outside
why can I just
never get over you
I miss you so bad
I miss us so bad
I just wish I didn't have to
mourn you while you're still here.

I want men

I want men to cower at my feet
when I walk past in my
morning clothes when I've
just rolled out of bed
and I've ran to the shop for some
orange juice with my pancakes
that I should've ate at 9am
but now it's half past 12
and little did I know but
men will still find me attractive
when my hair is in a
messy bun and it's
not been washed in a week
because I have the golden
heart of a saint
who would take bullets for
strangers or even foes.
sometimes people
don't hate you for your looks,
and maybe that because you have
A heart made of
soggy cardboard boxes

not an option

if you ever
think of picking me
as a last resort
or a second choice
remember
I am not an option.
I am the definite.
I should never be on the
checklist in your mind.
I am not something
you must think about
or something you're
not quite certain on.

-I am a definite.

Run Cold.

you are no longer my sunset
nor my sunrise
but the middle of the day when
I am lay in bed wondering
where I went wrong to believe
you were too good for the person
I have now grown into
And when I peeled back the curtains
It was often common to see
The sun still shone in and
Draws in lines on my skin
Which made me feel more loved.
More than you ever could
With words empty
And hearts run cold.
I don't need your warmth anymore
I've learnt how to do it myself.

blown out birthday candles
for another 365
and the smell of melting wax
with burning wicks
never fails to remind me
that yes, I am infact
another *365* closer to dying.

reflections of her figure
dance upon the walls
in forms of *shadows and silhouettes*
as she sings with her hairbrush
that she hasn't used in days
and the sounds echo round the room
as her little toes meet
with the cold laminate.
her nails painted and chipped,
her eyelashes filled with salty tears,
her voice all brittle and choked up
as she runs her fingers through her
knotted hair.
the floor covered in clothes
that she tried on and now
uses as a rug
in her little box room.
the sun is so warm
her life is so perfect
and the windows aren't open
yet she still feels the cold.

weed killer

please. for my sake.
leave me the fuck alone.
I am suffocating in a word that
somehow tangle me up in a past
I am no longer related to.
that. was. not. me.
I am not her.
i have grown into a
fearless woman who will
speak her mind.
not someone who was
afraid of breaking a heart
of a feeble boy who she was
no longer in love with.
I don't force my love anymore.
I don't fall for someone who
has a pretty face
with baby blue eyes
and a heart
which is patterned with danger.
I fall for souls. I fall for people.
I know who can catch me.
not people who would let me drown
in a rain shower
that could barely even
water the flowers
inside my heart.

weak independent woman

you wait for some type of
reassurance
from running your hands
over my greyish skin.
as though your wandering fingers
are supposed to make me feel
safe almost
yet I can't understand
why you'd believe that I'll
cower at your knees
believe that I
wear what I wear for your pleasure.
I dress how I like,
and I obey to those I chose.
you are not my muse
and I will happily live
without you in my life.

no, I'm not carsick
it's a little strange that
you're asking
if I get carsick a little
or a lot?
you're *multitasking*
thinking about my safety
and driving in your car
but we're not seeming to
go anywhere.
seems we're not making it
very far.
I pulled up the handbrake
on whatever we have
going on.
I'm not longer interested;
I don't want to meet your mum.
I guess I'm still not ready.
I'd like to take a break,
from this little three week meet up stage
and tell you that
I'm a broken part
that your car doesn't need.

I am my own
breath of fresh air
at *6:27am*
as I lie awake
with your arm
underneath me
as though you had built me up
yet I am hollow
and nothing but another
trophy for yourself
to use
and push around
as though I'm just a
doll you can
throw around.
I. am. not. your. muse.

thought we'd agreed to say
I love you even when the times
we're rough. but even when we
argue it's always me fixing it up
and at times I feel like you don't
care and it's only me that bothered
when it's a simple mixed
understanding yet I always come
out to *look like the bad guy.*

her youth just taken
she's only thirteen
but she was so young,
and pretty and lean
but her troubled life
had come too soon
she'd stay in bed
from dinner till noon
and she told herself
that calories are bad
but she knows inside
she's no longer sad
when she sees a meal
that she knows she doesn't want
instead says that she's ill
to avoid the resteraunts
it's *a strain in her brain*
but she sees the end goal
of being pretty and thin
but again, she now knows
that her parents got the hint
that she's no longer eating
she's instead all full up
from social media tweeting
as there's pictures of girls
who have Botox and filler
but she thinks that it's real
and *that's really the killer*
but yes, she was beautiful
before this had happened
she is beautiful still
her mould is just now a little patterned.

Emily Donoher

I would sacrifice my everything
to be how you are
the way you look
the way you write
every move you make
is so elegantly inspirational
you give me hope in
this world of misery
so please
whenever you feel you need
find relief in my hard times
when you compare
your life to mine
and see that yours is simply perfect
to the horror I have been through
and learn from my mistakes
as though I am your teacher
and you are my student
you deserve to understand
the beauty that
comes after the pain.

I guess I play the wallows
when I want to think of you
I think I need another sign
to tell me that we're through.
I am needing just a little more
to push me to the edge
in need of something
that will make me pledge
to never talk to you again
block your number from my phone
give me some sort of sign
to tell me you are not my home.

I know it's just a phase
you're not in love with me
you're searching for her
in the outfits I wear
but little do you know
my complexion
is a little lighter
and my hair
a little darker
you want to call me
by her name
as you lean against a barrier
stuttering out only letters
because you're a *drunken fool*
who can't string together
a sensible sentence.

2019.

you can be tired of the
way that people treat you
while you stick around because
you think you can't do better
and you deserve nothing but
a boy who will lie and a
boy who will make excuses
and make you feel like he's
giving you the world when he's
really giving you heartache
and a plain bowl of pasta.

what if I didn't react how I did
what if I told you
I didn't want to see you anymore
and said that I never wanted you to
step near me with your
lies and unfaithfulness of
the words you spoke that
you'd *rehearsed and*
engraved into your book of lies
that you'd told them same lies
infact so often that you
began to believe them
yourself as true
and you no longer know
how to be honest
with anyone.

You warm my hands, even when yours are cold. You giggle when I pull silly faces at you when you're driving and I'm in the back seats. You love to watch me do daily activities even if I pretend I don't notice you doing it. Maybe, just maybe, you're obsessed with me like I am with you. Maybe, just maybe, you see the potential in what we have, and you want that forever like I do. Truth is, *I want you around always,* I don't want to have to go a day without seeing your smile or your texts not reaching my phone, I want to laugh at pocket burgers and I want to be silly with you in the bath while we drink prosecco and laugh about our lives, I want to belly cry while you ice skate at Christmas, I want to be able to have our first experiences together, meet my extended family, have you round to see my little cousins, come to games nights, soirees at bars, late night drives, staying in our favourite countries together, everything in between. I am fascinated by you and I don't think I could ever live my life without you in it.

Les Fleurs

isn't it ironic?
how some people
will makes mere efforts to
mirror your lifestyle?
want what you want.
want what you have.
but that's it honey,
some people wish SO much
that they could be like you
and begin to dress like you,
act just as you would act
that they lose themselves in
who they actually are
because they're so hooked on
transforming themselves to
exist just how you exist.
it's okay to not feel guilty
when others do you wrong
because you're too good of a person
to think otherwise.

I don't know if these emotions are my own

or if I stole them from the person I have begged to
become
I don't know if these emotions are real
or if they're what I've created from sad stories,
poem books, my friends, movies on tv.
I don't know if I'm even me anymore
i don't recognise myself in the mirror
and if I rub my eyes hard enough
I see fragments of who I really am
scattered into flicks that disguise themselves
as tiny little stars of static
that stain my eyes when I open them after
I wish I knew who I was
I wish I understood myself properly.
-who's emotions are mine?

I am trying to choose to keep kind towards things that have been unkind to me. I never thought I'd be a forgiver *or* a forgetter however recent lights have really changed my perspectives on how I can make myself into a better communicator – I've learnt to own up to my mistakes, learnt how to be kind to myself, be nicer to others and be vulnerable to those I love. I realise we can't always uphold these mantras that we shout from rooftops and praise through churches, sometimes we must choose to break the cycle and follow what is best for ourselves – not just those around us. We must put ourselves in a risky situation to realise what we truly want and would take bullets for; we must see it from someone else's perspective. We can't always be perfect, and that's why *I am no longer choosing to be kind to unkind things.*

Sometimes I miss the way things used to be. The way I didn't have money struggles, how I didn't worry about what I ate or drank, I could let every weight off my shoulders when I danced, feed birds and pick flowers from neighbouring gardens. I never had to think that my actions had consequences, but once I knew and began to realise, they did, I stopped everything I loved in fear I would hurt someone. In fear I'd lose people that I loved, in fear they'd go and never come back, in fear id be alone. I hate being alone, I feel so much safer when I'm being protected. I am a weak soul who can only thrive around those who thrive, so when I'm alone my thoughts eat me alive. I don't want to be eaten alive. *I want to live.*

HOLDING ON

*Days I dwell on the past, I hold onto these memories
as memoirs of people I once but no longer know,
people who shaped me into the person I am today,
people who at one point in my life meant a lot to me,
who held my hand in the hardest moments, wiped my
tears when I cried and made me stronger every
second I spent with them. People who made
hurricanes of my world and then cleaned up with
kisses.*

10pm turned to 2am

It's only 10pm
it was as though a few cuddles
and kisses
and long conversations
allowed us to be vulnerable with each other
but in a way I couldn't speak to anyone else.
the warmth of your skin
making warmth in my lips
and it was as though
I couldn't help but stay away from you.
It's strange because it's not been long
and although I want you to stay the night
it's too hot inside and
I don't want to put any type of pressure on you.
and now I want you here all the time
to be able to smile and laugh with
being silly together is
all I could ever ask for.
laying kisses on my head
whilst your fingertips outlined my bra.
and it was as if I had blinked
and it had
turned to 2am.

I remember the first time I understood the meaning of skin aging. it was summertime and warm and the sun danced onto the mirror of the bathroom. I met this girl who I really got along with, and she stayed at a place with some of our mutual friends. We stayed the night so peacefully; she was 7 years older that I was, and I had never met someone who had made me feel this safe. I remember waking in the morning and washing our faces together, brushing our teeth and giggling in the process. Every time I caught a glimpse of her while doing so, I really saw the meaning of skin ages. *her smiles created creases,* but happy creases, signs that she had a good belly laugh in my company. signs that made her scowl and silly things I said. Signs she was aging well. And she was doing it happily. She deserved to stay beautiful, and she still is, but it clicks me sometimes that her lines were filled with love and laughter and rejoice instead of being filled with frowns and tears. That girl really made my smile creases bigger, made me cheese uncontrollably to the point my cheeks hurt, smile so much that she hurt me so bad, yet I still forgave her because I care for her. I'm glad she left lines for me.

it's 1:26pm as the
blazing sun kisses my skin;
burning.
sharp stubble scratches too,
but your lips
manage to heal the pain
with every kiss you place
so gently on my reddened shoulders
somehow have plastered the wounds
that I have to call my past
allowing me to see that
not all men are devils.
not all men are affectionless.
not all men are out to get me.
but most of all,
not all men are like him.
some men are like you,
yet you are you,
and you are almost perfect.
-green watch

And I Beg

oh, I wish you cared for me
the way I cared for you.
I wish you sat up at night
and cried as I do
feel the tears well up
at the tops of my eyes
as I dab my eyes dry
with the corner of my duvet
and I beg you to love me
and give me the time
that I give to you
when you don't even want it.
you wanted nothing but
someone to stroke your hair at night
until you fell asleep.
someone you would treat
and someone who would be
wrapped around your little finger
just because you could.

51 Manor Road

there's still imprints
where your coat was hung
shoes were slung
the things I'd do
to touch your skin
sing merry Christmas to you
you'd be in the family home
(you could even have my room if you wanted).
if there was ever a choice to
swap myself out for you,
I would've taken it in a heartbeat
because mum still struggles to smile
when its daffodil season,
and I can't shift the feeling
of missing your presence
wherever I go,
I always sit down and wonder
if you ever thought
I would be the girl that I've grown into.
-51 manor road

I crave my skin
to constantly smell
as though I've been
sat in your arms for hours on end
because I don't want to leave
just yet.
I want to jet wash your car
in the pouring rain
and lose the keys
all over again.
I want to make
silly, silly excuses
to see you,
telling you I need new shoes
maybe I want to go shopping, again.
or you're simply getting money
from the cash machine;
I'm coming along for the ride.
all for the reason
I want to sit
in your lil black box
with your hand
on my thigh
just so that
my skin can
smell of
you.

I'm addicted to the past as though it is a line of illegal substance, id swap my money for memories, hold onto it and soon after dwell. I can't clear my mind free of any life events, I can't get the idea of erasing, I can't delete pictures, I can't get out of my head. I'm sat wishing my life away on things that I can't change, I feel as though my life goes on, but I'm sat still begging the past will stay with me. I'm too busy moping over the past I never am able to recall what the present even looks like, as though my clubs of memories have been hoovered from the carpet I call my brain. *I don't know who I am anymore.* I am constantly living in my memories and never having the opportunity to make new or more.

So let me again

Feed you a chip over a FaceTime call
While we drunkenly confess our love at
3am when the sky is dark
And the room feels as though
It is spinning with the waltzers.
I miss you holding back my hair
When I'm being sick and telling you sorry
But not in the way that I needed your support
But in the way that you showed me love
That I have always wanted,
And that I deserved it too.

Baked Alaska

it's as though
it was only yesterday
you walked up
the path of my garden
and dropped off
some baked alaska,
and when you got home
you called me for hours
and we'd talk about your job
about my job
in the car,
on the way home,
when we wake up,
before we fall asleep.
my world simply
revolved around you
so, isn't it crazy?
how after a playlist of
good mornings
I simply became
another unlistened to track.

isn't it weird how little moons
have turned into supersonic stars
and now not only are we
just friends, but best friends
in something that is out of this world
and as the sun sets whilst we drive
down the M1 in the pitch black
blanketed by the stars that we chased
for little moons at Tesco's
and although it's dark now
you manage to brighten the mood
with the smile you leave me with
now I'm manifesting more of the
late night motorways
your hand on top of mine whilst
my skin feels cold but
I'm warm
warm from your kisses
on my small, small hands
as you twiddle with my thumbs
as you're about to change gears
because were taking a detour
we don't want to go home yet
so, we sit and stare at the
blanket of stars that
shower the skies like
sprinkles of glitter
and it was this one time that
led me to believe - you're my human.

she's so lovely, you sing it to me
whilst you drive down the m6
singing very off key in your
little Vauxhall Corsa
and even though we spend every little
second of time together
a fraction of glimpses that I catch
when you look over your shoulder
looking to reverse into the
parking spot outside my house
as though you want to
come inside and stay the night
but we both know we can't
and that's alright because one day maybe
just. maybe.
we will be growing up where we're
still in touch and we still have laughs
and still have the love
that we had or still have
the cold nights of 21's
because at the end of the day
we are still, and only ever will be.
– *alla tombe*

greedy for time
so, I take pictures of
everything from the
funny spilt orange juice
down the side of the fridge
to the way you
pick four leaf clovers
wherever we go
and you only ever find the ones
with three leaves (but I'll let you off).
pictures of the sunset
with sushi in our hands
and it's hard but
I'm greedy for time
I want to take the moment
and clip it in a
Chinese takeaway Tupperware tub
pop it in the fridge
and save the rest for
tomorrow.

your ghost

I knew this day would come
where you would fall out of love with me
but I didn't expect it to be so soon.
I expected you to still
kiss my forehead when you came home in the
mornings
and get butterflies when you see me
but instead, I'm like a ghost
sat in your cold bed sheets
and when you come home
you just must not see me
and I must just be nothing but
a mirage that is left from all the ideas
you had made up that I was
when I wasn't.

we used to talk about doing it
but I guess we never did
we both said that we'd always wanted it
ever since I was a kid
we'd get all happy when we see it
everyone was jealous
I wanted to believe it
would be as good if it did happen
it had been months since we stopped talking
but then I saw you show it off
that you had really gone and got one
and I still had gone and not.
-motorbikes.

it could've been us.
I could still have you up till
4:13am
just rambling on about life
when you weren't so worried about
screen time and
catching fish.
when it wasn't so hard to
try keep you around when
you didn't want to be.
when it wasn't a chore for you
to text me back
or drive to see me.
when I wasn't *fighting*
for your attention-
begging for a goodnight message.
Damn. I liked you.
I really thought we might've worked out.

we would talk about
how cigarette smoke filling lungs
would kill us one day.
we would joke about how
how we would go out so much
it would bore us.
you'd always joke
saying you wish it would
and *we'd drink our drinks*
whether we wanted them or not
because we needed the pain of life
to start taking its toll on us.
but I've stopped both.
I quit drinking;
it wasn't helping.
I stopped putting flame to the fire;
I didn't regret it.
yet now my body is dead.
I hope you're glad
you got your wish.
-living without the addiction of you.

I slept in my clothes
still wearing yesterday's lipstick
pretty hurts still on repeat
little did I know
at the age of 14
I didn't even know what
troubles felt like
instead, I'd shame myself
for the way I looked
and being pretty doesn't hurt
when you have a
beautiful soul.

Serenade me with the way you talk,
Effortlessly simple and smart,
Have me giggling under my breath
(Not to be cruel, I'm just laughing)
Bore me about numbers, for you I can
Pretend I'm a little interested.
For you I promise I will
thank my lucky stars that we can spend
Even a moment alone together and
Capture that look of your cheeky smile
Whenever you catch a glimpse of us.

Whitewash walls
Cream colour carpets
Cleaned ten times over
Still managing to hold
Mess from my childhood,
My adulthood,
Decades of laughter,
Decades of tears,
Spillages.
To those who come from the outside,
It's just a house.
From those inside,
We wouldn't change the carpets
For the world.

I hope he always gets to sleep
with the cold side of the pillow
and when I cannot close my eyes
I hope he sleeps nice and peaceful
when I wake up, he's always
tucking my hair behind my ears
and he's kissing on my forehead
and he's done it all these years
and even though we fell apart
we repaired every little thing
from the way we hold our hands
to the way we always bring
childish smiles to our faces
and we laugh until we cry
but the tears are always happy
and we're never asking why
we lost each other back then
because *we always knew*
that we'd find each other again
because we know it's true.
you're the one that I love
I can feel it in my heart
and although we spent time away
I never want time apart.

that first kiss
when we get out of these
invisible jail cells
will change everything.
all the hell we have been through
will slowly fade from our lives.
plans for afterwards
have already been made
so that I can taste your smile.
I have longed
for the moment
that our hands touch
and I don't have to be afraid
that we could both be endangered.
please now we're free
show me that you want me
and I promise
I will always be closer to you
and take advantage of the fact
we no longer have to be 6 feet apart.
-spring of 2020, lockdown.

walking the long way
just to see you
every minute I waste
is worth it for the second's taste
of your messy morning hair
and your joggers that are
halfway tucked into your socks
(although you'd never admit it)
and I can't even say
that I look any better
the smell of bleach
embedded into a
£15 pair of Slazenger's
that we can both laugh about
because not only are they
far from trendy
but they're bloody atrocious
but at least they're only work shoes.

I don't know what it is
about his voice
that's smooth as butter;
liquid gold.
letters of simplicity
draped in finery
disguised as poems
an architect of his own words
                    -Greek god

I'm lay contemplating
trying to convince myself
that you're not interested
in a little taste of
the past again
and even though
my mind aches for it
begs for it
dies for it
I probably shouldn't
be having these thoughts of
being in your arms
kissing me in the darkness
sneaking into your house
making me yet again late for work.

I want to feel as loved
as when you'd go
for a toilet break at work
just to text me back.
I want to feel as loved
as when you'd drive to me
at 6am
just to be my ride home.
I want you to love me
like you did
before you loved me
like you didn't
and left without explanation
to remember the time
you drove to my house
to give me a meal
for our virtual date
and the time you
decided it was time
to make me a
good morning playlist
ah, the things I'd do to
have you like I thought I did

in quarantine
times doesn't exist.
a cough is simply
a death warrant at your door
telling you that your life now consists
of not seeing the outside world
for two weeks
as you could be a carrier.
I can't remember a time
when your arms were not labelled
as a danger zone
but the day the chain is broken
and we all learn to keep it under control
hugs and kisses will no longer be
signing away a life of a loved one.
we will simply never appreciate
something more than
the life we have been given.

Always You.

In constant awe of everything you do
I want to touch your skin but all the time,
Let you stroke the sides of my face
Trace the freckles on my cheeks
That constantly hurt from smiling at you,
You bring out my happiest self and I
Can't help but ugly smile around you every time
You give me the eyes,
Across the table, in the kitchen, in the coffee shops.
Working things out maturely
Made us realise what a good team we make.
Were like bonnie and Clyde but
Modernised,
Salt and pepper but
More flavourful.
Lemon and lime but
Sweeter.
Match made in heaven you could say.

I'm now lay in arms
that are not yours
as they pull me closer
but it's the tears that
are in the brink of my eyes
that are making this harder
and *I wish it was you*
who was wiping my tears
but instead, he is much smaller
and he doesn't cry
and I don't think he ever will
his past has him building walls
that he is never willing to take down.

laughing twice as loud
just so I hope that you hear
and think that you are
better off without me but I know
you don't want to squash your own pride
and instead, you'll use me
as your limbo when it hits
12pm and nobody's here
and you'll want me to
talk the truth
when you couldn't even say hello
and it hurts my heart so bad because
I can't beg you to stay
but at the same time
I don't want to have to
beg you to leave either
I thought that you'd be my one
forever but instead I'm now
being nobody's one and I'm
alone on this
freezing cold
September night
wishing that you'd come say hello instead of
staring at me across the room
and I just feel SO awakened
knowing you want every single person
that isn't me
-regardless of what you said
you really hurt me
whether it was intentional or not.

I've dug my nails into my palms so hard it's created little crescents in my skin

I wish you never made me feel so much anger
I wish it didn't creep up on me like a cold night in
July after it's been sunny all day
I wish I knew instead of just catching the shock from
finding out over the phone
we were an electrical circuit, together we could
power the world
but without you? I'm nothing.
I beg you to love me again
I beg and I beg and I beg
i miss you so much
so much, that all it does is ache.

train station kisses

as I kiss you right here
I know for a fact that
there's so many more *train station kisses*
to come for us
where I'll have to watch you leave
and vice versa
where we come back to our
empty beds and talk as
though we're still here
playing Mario kart at
5pm when it's still light outside
and leaving when we're 2 drinks down
and it's dark outside
and I want to hold your hand
I really do want to hold your hand
but mine are shaking from nerves
because you make me
quite literally
weak at my knees.
I'll tie your shoes 100 times over
and get gluten free menus
and have the *train station kisses*
        -if it means you'll stick around.

You got rid of me and let me back into your life. I begged at your knees for what felt like a lifetime. I cried in your bed, I sobbed in your arms, I stopped eating and abused myself in malicious ways and drove myself clinically insane. It was funny really because a week or two later you did the same. You left me again. I guess that makes me twice as lucky to get away from you more than the once. I was blinded by a person that you weren't, but a person that I wanted you to be.

- sadly, you're not that person anymore

Teatime
/ˈtiːtʌɪm/

Verb

    - I had an ex and I adored that human more than life itself, we used to do this thing every Sunday where we'd make a cup of tea and put our phones in the kitchen and leave them there on charge, go into living room / bedroom / dining room / garden and spend quality time together. It's something unique that I've never done / never will do with anyone else, every time I link something to that specific event example having a cup of tea and not being on my phone or sitting in the garden and just watching the sky. It does bring back feelings. The feelings aren't always feelings of love and lust, because during teatime we didn't always see eye to eye. We had argued previously during teatime, so sometimes I'd get feelings of upset / anger. This doesn't mean the passing feelings mean I want him back, because it's more of a bittersweet idea every time I pick up a coffee mug.

Cutting corners

I don't even care that
Anyone else is in the room right now
Because it's my hand you're holding
While the tv plays in the background
And my fingers tease your hair
As you sleep like a baby
Tucked between my legs.
I don't even feel afraid anymore
Because I wish it was just us
In my bed this time, not here
So, I could tell you how pretty you really are.
I don't want to leave in the morning
I want you to stay around a little longer
Or come over again sometime
You're my favourite friend
But favourite is such a weak word
For how you made a spark inside me light
That I thought was physically impossible
And I thought it had died.
-if this is the last time I see you,
Ill regret it forever

You leave me on a natural high
I feel so elated when I'm around you
your hand rests on my leg
as I drift off on your warm blanket
your hair is a little longer
softer
and I want to stay here all night
while I sit and stare at your ceiling
instead of mine
because I feel so safe in your company
and I know I can call you at any time.
your *vinyl players spinning*
and playing songs we love
songs I love that you love
you see you creep up like a cold night
and I don't know how to stop that
because sometimes I don't want to leave
sometimes I just want to stay with you.

I don't like
the you that you've turned out to be
it's not you I know, or knew
and it's sad to see you like that,
I guess I'll never know who
you really are
and it's sad that I'm afraid that
I don't know who you are.
your lies mislead me into darkness
and now I'm sat alone
no mop stick microphones
no trolly runs.
alone.

Heated blankets

We alight even in the darkest of places
As we laugh about pain and tragedy
As though were in a science lecture
Because we care but we don't,
And how you make me laugh
Until my chest hurts,
Not chest pain, no 999.
You make me smile when I'm miserable,
You make my cheeks hurt actually,
you're so silly yet so pretty
And I am in awe of your beauty
Even if you don't see it.
I think you're like, so cool,
But I don't know if it's too much
To tell you that because
I don't want to overstep any unspoken boundaries.
We're supposed to be besties so
I can tell you anything so
Please pinky promise
That you'll never tell a soul
If I confess things I have in the
Back of my mind
That are written on reems of paper
Shaped like cut out gingerbread men.

The butterflies are knives,
Every thought I have of you tears me up on the
inside
Because these thoughts
Shouldn't be what I'm thinking of
Thinking of you and me together
Thinking how perfect we could be together.
We could be together.
But we can't and I could
Never tell you that because these thoughts loom
In the depths of my heart as we
Hold hands and play with each other's hair.
We can't be together I know that
But it doesn't mean I don't think about it
Every single time I sit with you,
Laugh with you,
Cry with you,
Eat with you.
I think of you so much
And I should probably just stop thinking
Instead, I should erase you and I from my mind
With a dishcloth and soap
But all I think of is
Re writing our names over and over
Until the pen runs out.

I still have the video of you singing
Bohemian rhapsody at new year
(new year you bought me sparklers)
And I still hope to the life of me
That is still your karaoke song because
That night I smiles till my cheekbones
Almost dropped off. Oh,
My little babisko I really hope
That you still think of me from
Time to time even though I was
An awful person to you and you will
Always deserve better than me.
I still love you and
I still miss arguing about moam rappers with you
You were my favourite ex and
I think you always will be.

FORGIVING AND CHOSING KINDNESS

Days I have forgiven those who have hurt me, allowed my feelings to not take over how I act as a person and not react negatively to things that would've once hurt me. Choosing kindness over choosing to be closed off and unforgiving allowed me to grow as a person and mature at a young age. Days I have forgiven in order to help me grow my relationships, friendships, opportunities and allowing soul healing.

I don't know if I want to kiss your lips
just so I can taste her
and see how it would be
to be with someone who
prepped her lips like
a wedding reception
and washed herself in
the finest of gold
as though she was hand carved
by worker bees
or hand made
by a jeweller.
she was formed with
crystals
and her diamond eyes,
fragile soul,
poor girl.
I can show her
what love really feels like.

As we head to the horizon of another year of our love, I look back on all the challenges we've faced together, all the fallouts, the hard times, the months of separate growth, the love we have shown and warmth we've had in our hearts for each other. You bring me happiness when I'm down, smiles when I feel like crying and you tease your fingertips on my back when I'm drifting off to sleep. Truth is you're the only person I want to wake up to in the mornings, the only person who makes me feel like a human, special notes you leave me before work, before I get to spend another entire day laughing with you, singing our favourite songs on full blast driving down winding country roads. You complete parts of me i didn't realise were empty, you enlighten me with things I didn't realise I didn't know, and you fill my soul with utter bliss. Thank you for another 365 of learning how to love me. Thank you for letting me love you.

-a year of us

why

so why does it still feel like
you're still here when I'm
not near you and I
can't touch your skin
to be able to feel that
you are infact real
and instead I'm relying on
social media to tell me
that you're okay.
I should be
asking you with words that
I want to say but i know
I don't have a pass to
double text you anymore.
-I hope you sorted yourself out
a phone charger

I never asked or
wanted anything from you
but you left a mark that
I can't just erase anymore.
god I love you.
i adore each 206 bones
in your body,
the *freckle in your bellybutton,*
even when you struggle to.
your smile is contagious
and the mark has been left
on my life that
you so peacefully made.
I just love you so much
that it is physically painful
to not love you anymore.

and I know that I'm not her
but I can try and mean something to you
whether that's someone you can message
call me baby over the phone before I leave
to then sit and wonder where you went wrong
in your single bed down on Middleway view
whilst you stroke your own hands
and you sing your own songs
instead of having her there to protect you.
I am not her. and I can never replace that feeling.
but I can try.

jealousy disguised as *fragile smiles*
almost as though I'd been
crying all night for
karma to get me.
like I said I'm sorry
only I should've never thought that from you
when I did and I don't know why
never did I think you would do that
don't get me wrong
everyone has tried to convince me
something was always special between us
I was just blind sighted by the light.

walking the long way
incase you'd see me after work
suddenly became
messaging your phone to
meeting you at your car
then it was days out that
turned to travelling with you
tucked under covers
late night conversation
next to you
I'm in your arms
when it falls to dusk.
now that I'm yours,
I walk the long way,
this time with your company
just so I get a moment more
to catch a last kiss
or see your *hazel eyes* shine.
it's crazy how
you can get what you want
when you can eventually
stop doubting yourself
and realise you deserve
the happiness you receive
from someone, who although
is way out of your league,
treats you like you are the
only person they can see.

I stay around and this time
It's not just because I want you in my life
But I'm somehow magnetised to your
White lies.
I thought it really could've fixed the
Perspective of life that
I had stuck on
Being heartbroken
I wish everything hadn't gone on
And that it was just
Black and blue.
Me and you.
It must have been
An April fool's day joke
However, I thought that
Jokes were supposed to
Make me laugh until
I'm sick on the floor.
    -all I did was cry until I couldn't breathe.

I Wish.

I wish you loved me the way I loved you
I wish you missed me
I wish you came where you know I am
I wish I wish *I wish* I wish.
and I will keep wishing
until one day you come back to me
and I know I let you go
and now
only just now
I wish I never let you go
because
I wish that I could trust you
and we both know my trust is very fragile.
you tampered a little too hard
the shards shattered in my hands
getting under my skin
why could you not love me
I wish that you would just love me.

aged like dirty beer

some things scar more than others
we idolise those
who are older
more wise
we trust those who
birth us
yet let them
critically analyse
every one of our actions
yet we say it's because they
'know better'
when it's just because
we know worse.

I am holding to the past
as though my future depends
on everything I have lived through
everything I have overcame.
rope burns cover my palms
yet we cover them in aloe vera
and kiss them better
with beer tainted breath
and ruby stained lips.

the delicacy of feeling
was never a low when
I could always sense your
hands on my waist
or in my hair
I could feel your
hot breaths against
my cold neck when it's
3am and the
tv is muted
but when it's 1pm you
never seem to cross my mind
so why do you
only linger at the night-time
when your
words are split into syllables
and your brain
wouldn't even think of me
in ways that
I think of you.
I don't beg you to love me anymore
but I beg you to stop
hiding in the shadows in my heart
and peeking through the
depths of my thoughts
get your hands
off what is no longer yours.
nobody is to blame,
but if I had to put it onto someone,
it'd be you.

I've imagined us meeting again
so many times over that
it has made me convince myself
that you're coming back for me
even when I know deep down
you're not.
I have a feeling that even though
we're not even acquaintances anymore
if I was to ring you at early hours
when the sun has only just
started to rise upon the hills
that we once sat upon
you'd instantly pick up your phone
and make sure you called me back
even just for 5 minutes
to make sure I'm okay.

I can't wait to fall out of love with you.
I dream it in my lonely bed
while I know you're out in the clubs
touching other girls, kissing other girls
telling them you're available
when we all know you're not emotionally.
I can't wait for you to understand
the truth of a heartbreak
how it feels to break someone else's heart
you'll finally be in my shoes
I hope they're tied incredibly tight.
I can't wait for you to be gone from my life
where you no longer loiter in passing memories
and I no longer rely on you to save me
I will learn time save myself
even if it's the only thing I can do to help myself.
yet I will wait forever
to fall back in love with you again.

one thing loss taught me
is that you cannot just bandage
over a wound that needs stitching.
you cannot just replace
what has gone.
you cannot just tell yourself
that everything is okay
and not let out how you feel.
it is okay to cry
and allowing yourself
to become your emotions
and feel how you feel
instead of convincing yourself
that you are fine
when in reality all you want
is another hug.
a second chance.

I never wanted us
to end like this
and it's sad because I
just believed so hard
as though I was about to
fly off to wonderland
but instead, I was
left broken
torn up on the fact
we could never
keep truthful between each other
and I quite frankly
never wanted us to end.
we can only say sorry
so many times, as we
scream songs in the
wrong pitch and tune
because we need to
get things off our chest
but it soon came to me
that we weren't getting
anything off our chest
apart from each other
-I hope you find happiness in someone else

I say, that's fine with me
as you rest your hand
on the bottom of my back
I nod my head
when you lead in to kiss me
but you don't close your eyes
until you've visually seen
me confirming you can.
but isn't it funny how I'm now
tangled in your big lie.
it doesn't bother me. it never did.
but I never said yes to the person you are
I said yes to the person I thought you were.

Room Share.

Caitlin Alice Slann, our childhood consisted of us constantly fighting over minor things such as me wearing your clothes (which I definitely did do), stealing your perfume and wearing your socks. But as we've grown, I've realised how petty it all was. If you rang me at any time of the day, asking to borrow something now, I'd never say no to you. You're my big sister and as we have now grown older, you're my best friend and I don't know what I'd ever do without you. I want to say that I forgive you for tormenting me as a kid, I always love that you would always give me advice even if I never followed it and you were such a role model to me growing up. You are my rock, and without you on this world I would be the saddest little sister alive, thank you for everything you've done for me, and I forgive you for helping me character build as a child.

I've not felt myself in months, weeks, years. I don't know where I went, i was so all for life but I just lost it. I lost stimulation, work ethic, will to live, willpower to carry on. it sucks. everything. sucks. I fail to feel happy day in, day out, I beg myself better and I wipe my tears with hope I won't cry tonight. I try to fix myself when I catch peeks of my golden skin being kissed by dimmed sunrays, I forgive myself for feeling this way, I repair with every compliment and every conversation. but I'm still not myself, no matter how much makeup I wear, how much I work out, how much I sleep in a day, how healthy I eat. I am just not myself. *I. am. lost.*

dependency

you were a quick fix
and now I don't have
you to rely on anymore
I feel lost in this world.
I don't know how I can
manage to feel like me
again, without going
back to you for a small
rush or just a temporary
buzz to feel like I'm on
top of the world, when
in reality, I am sliding
myself into relapse in
choosing to give in to
the devils, that tell me
to take you for breakfast
and skip meals for you.

instead, day in, day out
I push away the relapse
and battle against the
bad, to try and find me
amongst the high that
you wound give me whilst
I'm alone in my room with
nothing but the lights out
and the music loud, just
staring into the stream
of sparkle on the walls that
was reflected light onto the
bathroom mirror which would
tell me I should
abuse a bag of
bad decisions, which I
knew wasn't following
the satnav that's set
destination was to lead
to recovery road.
-recovery isn't linear, it's in waves

I don't miss you like I used to miss you. I won you back and now I have you it was nothing like I pictured, you're not the same person I met a year ago. You're not the same you, you don't like the same things, or laugh like you used to, and although that hurts maybe it means that I should *let you go* instead of wishing you'll somehow turn back into the person you once were. I don't want to beg you or cry in the bathroom on the floor anymore, I don't want to have to feel like I need to earn you or win you over. I shouldn't have to fight for your attention while you play the PlayStation, I shouldn't need to. You should admire my presence at least every moment you have free, but you don't, you check your phone for other girls and you wish your days away from me come sooner. I'm tired of pretending you're still you. You were never the person I thought you up to be.

it looked so fun to smile with you

and when I smiled with you
(at you)
in the car mirror fixing your hair
trying to fold up my underwear
looking at my bum in my denim flares
and you can't help but stop to stare
at the person you smiled at
and truly ever meant to show your
smile too because you didn't want it to be me.
I know who you pretend I am
she was never me.

But I could never be mad,
Because when I smile with you,
It hurt my cheekbones so much that I
Forget that I would be broken
If this was to ever end.

we live like Tetris

we sleep in a perfect formation,
Your hand sits in mine as though they were
Made for each other, we're in sync,
Our similarities so different yet we
Live alongside each other so peacefully
You know what I like, and I know
Exactly what you like too.
Just like that.
I wish the world didn't pull us apart,
The imputs from friends and the
Weight of our own lives
Didn't damage our already broken seams,
I wish you never had to
Kiss someone else but if that means
It'll bring you back to me,
Then kiss your frogs,
Sell your soul to demons,
Spend a night with someone else
If that will ever make you realise
That we live like Tetris
And nobody else will fit
Just quite like me and you do.

Time after time I'm getting my heart ripped out by people who want nothing but temporary love, nobody in the world wants anything to do with me more than my body for a night, and its breaking me down so much its actually rather humorous now I think of it. You hurt my heart 100x over and I forgive you because I love you, I ignore red flags disguised as questioning thoughts, I pretend I don't see things that I watched you do, I hide my eyes if it's something I want to see but know my stomach would never forgive me because it would refuse food and bring up everything that even touches the lining of the tummy. You brew my blood to boil, and I can't get this theory out of my head that I was an easy place for you to trauma dump and have someone to go through things with, and once you were done you left me in the dirt to rot.

-*you wanted someone better but didn't have enough time to find her, so you settled.*

QUESTIONING

*Days I have questioned who I am, what I am here
for, why I exist. Turns out you don't need to
understand your own existence in order to live. Its
beneficial to question why we exist and why we take
risks in understanding ourselves and inquiring about
situations we find ourselves in.*

trust me, I see how you look at me
brushing my hair
getting changed in the mornings
towel drying myself
in the warmth of your room
I know how you look at me.
I know what you think of me,
I know how you react to some of my ideas,
but I know you don't really want rid.
babe? *it's me?*
don't leave me?
you said you wanted this?
I can't understand
how someone could walk out on something
that needed just a little
bit of tweaking?
when I see how you look at me
brushing my hair.
you still want me, don't you?

restless nights

it was strange because
I knew I loved you but
my nights seemed restless
because I needed to feel
you were there but you never
hugged me to sleep or
stroked my hair and it
made me feel hard to love
when I knew that I am
the most easiest,
most simplest form of human
that this world has ever seen
because I don't ask
for much of anything.
I don't want anything
materialistic from you,
instead, now
all it's done is made me question
why did you not love me?

something isn't right

I want to give you everything
but nothing at the same time
I'm scared of tying on to you
like a drowning child in a
freezing cold lake in the
middle of winter and I
don't quite know what it is
but I get good however mostly
bad vibes from the way you
are with me and maybe it's
because you're too nice and
you won't be cruel like everyone
else has been but in a way
it kind of scares me into
thinking because you're so nice
that something isn't right.

how do I know
if I feel what I feel
what if they're just attractive
I don't think that it's real
is it real?
or could I really?
things I guess I never know
and I try to hide the feelings
but sometimes I let them go
let them creep through
the holes in my heart
that couldn't take the pressure
of my confused emotions
yet here they are
buried deep like treasure.
feelings being dug up
from every cavern in my heart
I guess I know the feeling
when love is tearing me apart
I don't want people to judge me
I guess I think I'm built like this
I don't know if this is what I am
but I guess it's hit or miss.
-*girls*

time is money

did you just want a
new accessory on your arm
when the watches weren't enough
of the cuff links not fulfilling
did you just want me to
boost up your ego
an addition to the social status
is being with a pretty face
all you really wanted?
is there a single thing you
actually know about me
and I mean not just the colour of my eyes
or the way my thighs wobble when I walk
I mean my favourite food or
my favourite song.
I'm really not sure
if I can settle for you.

the answers were embedded
into your silence.
when I'd call for your help
with *silent signals*
you'd miss them all
as though you were an
elderly man
attempting to read a book
with words on pages
when you should be
reading braille.
as though you were a deaf man
trying to listen to
Bob Dylan through
a broken headset
and could feel the vibrations
of sound waves
but couldn't unpick the words
from the mumbled form of
noise.

whenever I was
in the vicinity
of your house
I would check the windows
of passing cars
to see if I could see you
driving past.
but now whenever I'm
around the area
that you live
I'm only checking for your car
to make sure that
you're not home.

You crashed your car today.
You were drunk driving.
I wish it had killed you.
You don't deserve to walk this earth.
You've been handed life on a plate,
Told to do whatever you want,
Taught how to be reckless,
Helped yourself out in ruining your life,
You've done some soul-destroying things.
You should be behind bars.
Yet you still walk around as though
You're the gift from god.
So, before you try to convince yourself
That you're a good person,
Think,
What would your mum do if
She knew you were a rapist?

I know he's falling
out of love
and every second
that we talk
he bats an eye
left on reply
for more than hours
at a time
and when I wake
he doesn't call
he doesn't text
he doesn't talk
now it's just
me and my emotions
trying to figure
what went wrong.
and I say
I'm overthinking
and it's in my head
but when it's ten past twelve
gone midnight
and I'm still sat in my bed
thinking what did I
do this time
to make you feel like crap
I guess I
sit and wonder
is this the time
you don't come back?

To try get close to you

Did you like how I dressed today?
I heard purple is your favourite colour.
The shoes I wore, yeah, they make
Me think of you for some reason.
Oh, you like how I laughed at your joke?
How about when I became friends with
Your friends, how we went out for pizza
And talked about our lives like
We'd known eachother for an eternity.
But that's okay. I shouldn't be thinking of you
But for some reason, you're the only
Thing that's in my head, the way you smile
And your eyes crease, the way you just
Know. You just. Know.

You swore on your life
that you hated that song
but the bar on the
right hand side
tells me you're repeating the past
repeating the song
now you've dragged me
through your shit
it looks like your still sat
listening to what you used to
hate
now laughing in my face.
because I used to comfort you
to what you called your own hell
now your sat singing it again as though
she had *cured the words*
and made them pretty again for you
what do you expect me to feel?

questioning

sorry I'm a little off,
I feel down today.
you probably already guessed?
I'm a burden, I get it.
I'm sorry about that.
I struggle to give you time to yourself
but that's just because I'm
scared of abandonment.
yes, I'm sorry
I should stop saying sorry.
but it's hard when
I feel like you ache with
every word you type to me
I know inside you're
tired of me
and I get it because I'm
tired of myself too.
but how can I apologise
without an s, an o, double r and a y?

something isn't right

I want to give you everything
but nothing at the same time
I'm scared of tying on to you
like a drowning child in a
freezing cold lake in the
middle of winter and I
don't quite know what it is
but I get good however mostly
bad vibes from the way you
are with me and maybe it's
because you're too nice and
you won't be cruel like everyone
else has been but in a way
it kind of scares me into
thinking because you're so nice
that something isn't right.

creases form at the sides of my eyes
you say stupid stuff
like sometimes really silly
but it's oddly funny that I laugh
and I laugh till my belly hurts
nobody should make me laugh
like you do but, you do
and it's weird
I don't like it
but I like it
and I like your company
and the stupid things that you say

maybe you'd be like a
birthday cake with sprinkles
orange leaves in autumn,
Storytime at night,
soft fuzzy socks.
but *I don't know what you think of
when you think of me?*

Stalling.

I often find myself stalling
Not because I don't know what to say
But I don't know how to say it
In a way you won't think I'm crazy
But I know you wouldn't think it's crazy
If I rang you at 3am to
Go on a drive while we sing our favourite songs,
Karaoke songs
I wonder if well ever meet again.
In a club on a weekday.
6 and a half years is a long time
If only we met in college,
But the weirdest part is
I think we may have hated each other
If we met back, then
Because I was never who you know me as now
But I wish we met sooner.
And in the future?
Maybe 6 and a half years will be nothing.
Who knows?

sobering up on your kisses,
when I should be tucked under
my blankets crying about you
yet here I am making the same mistake.
I keep pretending we can be just friends
but I can't do it for myself.
why when I try and move on
and have something going well
I able to hold back texting your phone
yet somehow, I'm bringing myself
back to you.
why am I still wanting you?
only when you're around
because without your messages to me
I am able to survive from
someone else's love.
(my own).
it's not that I regret it as such
but I wish we were both capable
of being just friends.
-*alcohol free beer.*

Why don't you try understanding me?
When I want to tell you how I'm feeling.
I wish you took a second of your day
To just look at how I look at you
In utter raw pain of your beauty
In awe of every dimple and crease.
You made me feel so invincible when she's around,
I know you're looking straight through me
Wishing it was her instead.
You'll be embarrassed if you know
How much I know and what I know.
Maddy really knew that you just wanted to
Fool me around and make me stick around
when the love is all gone.
-Hope he knows we're out tonight

Questioning your intentions
As we sit on the phone and you
Rate my outfit for the day
And I do really like you but
I think you know that it's nothing but
I wish that you were closer
And your promises weren't empty
Because it feels like I'm nothing but someone
That you text to pass your time
(even if I am)
I wish I wasn't left here guessing if you
Actually, want to meet me,
Take me for a coffee,
We can talk about our chaotic lives and how
Were both so busy we have no time to date,
(especially each other)
Our schedules will never
Work our Mr Wycombe,
But it doesn't mean I want to stop trying because
you
Somehow give me butterflies and I
Hate it yet it still makes me smile when you
Say I'll see you soon over texts.
- I wish you were a phone guy.

Printed in Great Britain
by Amazon